This book belongs to:

....

Written and edited by Susannah Bailey
Designed by Claire Cater and Jack Clucas
Cover design by Claire Cater

MY
TOPSY-TURVY
PUZZLE BOOK

Buster Books

First published in Great Britain in 2020 by Buster Books,
an imprint of Michael O'Mara Books Limited, 9 Lion Yard,
Tremadoc Road, London SW4 7NQ

With material adapted from shutterstock.com

W www.mombooks.com/buster   f Buster Books   🐦 @BusterBooks

Copyright © 2020 Buster Books

ISBN: 978-1-78055-706-9

1 3 5 7 9 10 8 6 4 2

This book was printed in August 2020 by Leo Paper Products Ltd,
Heshan Astros Printing Limited, Xuantan Temple Industrial Zone,
Gulao Town, Heshan City, Guangdong Province, China.

FSC
www.fsc.org

MIX
Paper from
responsible sources
FSC® C020056

INTRODUCTION

This book is full of puzzles where things are topsy-turvy
- upside down, the wrong way round, twisted, turned and
flipped. Can you solve them? All you need is a pen or a
pencil, and you're set for loads of topsy-turvy puzzle fun.

You'll find all of the answers at the back of the book.

So, what are you waiting for? Turn the
page to enter a topsy-turvy world!

LION PRIDE

Take a close look at this lion family. Can you **count** the number of cubs and **circle** who does **not** quite belong?

CHILLING OUT

These sloths are hanging about in the rainforest.
Can you **find six** differences between the two scenes?

SEASIDE SAILING

It's a beautiful day out at sea, but can you **spot** the **three** boats sailing in a **different direction** to the rest?

BLACK BATS

Look at this dark cave, filled with flapping bats. Which bat is the **odd one out**?

MONKEY SEARCH

Can you **find** the **three** monkeys that are swinging around **upside down**?

TRICK REFLECTION

Look at the houses, then look at their reflections in the water.

Can you **spot four** differences between the two?

HITTING THE SHOPS

The animals are in the fruit and veg shop. Can you **circle** the things that shouldn't be there? There are:

★ 8 shoes   ★ 5 doughnuts   ★ 2 books

LOTS OF LADYBIRDS

Can you **spot** a butterfly friend
among the ladybirds?

TASTY FRUIT

The fruit is in a muddle! Can you **match** each piece with its **partner**? **Circle** the fruit that does **not** make a pair.

FAIRGROUND FUN

The monsters are in the hall of upside-down mirrors at the fairground. Which mirror reflection does **not match** the monster?

SLITHERING SNAKES

These snakes are all jungle friends, but can you **find** the one with a **different skin pattern** to the rest?

BUTTERFLY FLUTTERBY

These butterflies have grown giant! Can you **spot**
the butterfly that's the **biggest** of them all?

HAPPY HORSE

Look at the horse and its reflection.

Can you **spot four** differences between them?

WRONG BABY

Uh-oh — the animal babies have been **swapped** around.
Can you **match** them back into baby-and-parent **pairs**?

SUPER SHADOWS

Look at the superheroes and their shadows.

Can you **match** each hero up with their correct **shadow**?

SNOWY SCENE

Snow has fallen! Can you work out which **two** pieces **fit** where to complete the scene? **Circle** the piece that does **not** belong.

JUMPER JUMBLE

Look at these wrapped-up rabbits. Can you **find** the one wearing a jumper with a **different pattern** to the rest?

LOOP THE LOOP

The pigs are having a day out at the funfair. Can you **spot** **six** differences between these rollercoaster scenes?

SWEET SEARCH

Look at all the crunchy, different-coloured apples.

Can you **find** the sweet hidden among them?

SCHOOLYARD SWAP

Can you **circle** the **five** things that are in the playground but should be in the **classroom**, and the **five** things in the classroom which should be in the **playground**?

FLYING AWAY

The animals are taking a spin in the sky, but which **three** planes are going a **different way** to the others?

CUDDLY CATS

These cute cats are relaxing. Can you **follow** the **lines**
to find out which ball of wool belongs to which cat?

TIGER TWINS

Can you **match up** the tigers into identical **pairs**?
Circle the tiger that does **not** have a twin.

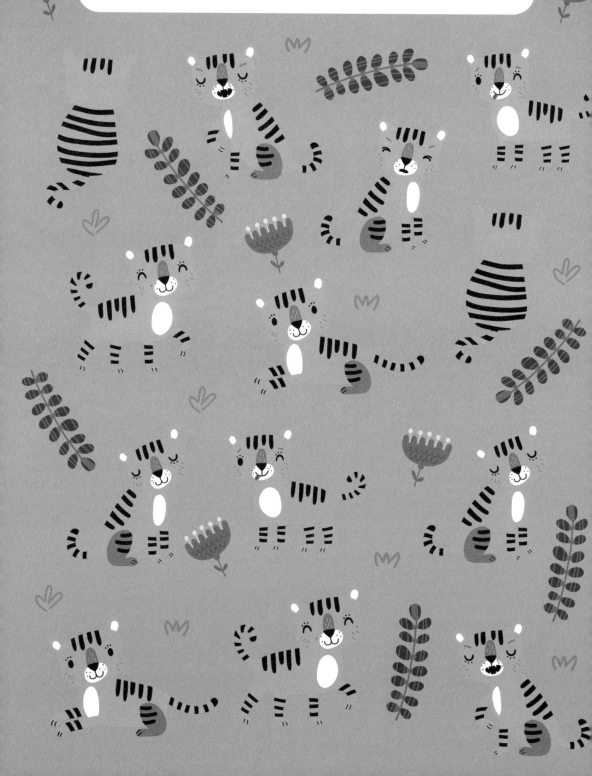

TINY AND TINIER

These elephants have shrunk! Can you **find** the one that's the **smallest** of the herd?

ON THE FARM

Look at all the cows in the farmyard. Can you **count** the baby calves and **circle** who does **not** belong on the farm?

POSING PENGUINS

The penguins are using their reflections to get ready for the day. Which reflection looks **different** from its penguin?

FOREST FINDINGS

How strange – this wood is full of creatures that usually live by the sea. Can you **circle** them? There are:

★ 8 penguins ★ 5 puffins ★ 2 walruses

ICE COLD

It's time for an ice cream! Can you **circle** the milkshake that has got mixed into the grid?

TEDDY TIDY

These teddies have been thrown about all over the bedroom floor. Can you **pair** them back up?

CAKE DROP

Oh no, the cake stand has fallen over! Can you **circle** these **three** cupcakes in the picture below?

CLIMBING CATS

The cats are having a party in the tree. Can you **count** the cats and **circle** the visitor who has come to join the fun?

FLAMINGO FLOCK

The flamingos have gathered in the water. Can you **circle** the reflection that has a **different shape** to its flamingo?

PANDA PAIRS

Look at all the playful pandas. **Sort** them into **matching pairs**, then **circle** the one that does **not** have a partner.

AT THE CIRCUS

It's time for the topsy-turvy circus! Can you **circle** the **three** animals that are upside down?

FLOWER POWER

Help the bee visit the flowers by **following** them in the **order** below. She can move up, down, left and right but not diagonally.

START

FINISH

BY THE SEASIDE

At the topsy-turvy seaside, there are **five** things on the beach that belong in the **sea**, and **five** things in the sea that belong on the **beach**. Can you **circle** them all?

IN A FLAP

The birds are flying away this winter, but which **three** birds are heading in a **different direction** to the rest?

FUN IN THE SUN

The llamas are out for a day in the desert.
Can you **match** each llama to its **shadow**?

ELEPHANT SPLASH

These elephants are having a water fight in the forest. Can you **count** the babies and **circle** who has come to visit them?

TONS OF TEAPOTS

The cats are laying out their tea sets.
Can you **spot** where they've put the cups?

MIRROR, MIRROR

The robots are having fun looking in the upside-down mirrors.
Can you **spot** which reflection has a **difference** in it?

IN THE TREETOPS

The birds are flying high! Can you **spot**
the **five** that are upside down?

BUSY BUGS

These insects are doing their daily exercises.

Can you **spot six** differences between the two pictures?

PARENT SWAP

These animals have all ended up with the **wrong** baby.

Can you **match** each baby back up with its parent?

ZEBRA HERD

The zebras are out and about. Can you **circle** the zebra that looks a little **different** to the rest?

JUST KEEP SWIMMING

It's time for school! **Three** fish are swimming the **opposite way** to the rest to get there. Can you **spot** them?

COLOURFUL CAMELS

The camels are taking a break in the desert. Can you **find** the one that looks **different** from its reflection?

FOLLOW THE FOOTSTEPS

The yetis are having fun in the snow. Can you **follow** the **footprints** to find out which child belongs with which parent?

MOUSE HOUSE

These houses are the perfect size for a mouse. Can you **find** the house that's the **smallest** of them all?

DIGGER DILEMMA

Can you work out which **two** pieces **fit** where to complete the scene? **Circle** the puzzle piece that does **not** belong at all.

TIME FOR TEA

The cakes are out and it's time for a tea party! Can you **spot six** differences between the two party scenes?

FOUR LITTLE PIGS

These pigs are looking in trick mirrors. Can you **spot** which reflection does **not match** its pig?

UNDER THE SEA

The sea is full of fish, but there are some other animals here as well that don't belong. Can you **circle** them? There are:

★ **8 mice** ★ **5 parrots** ★ **2 foxes**

LOTS OF SPOTS

The leopards are lazing about in the trees. Can you **find** the one with a **different-patterned** coat?

SPACE RACE

The aliens are whizzing back to their homes in the sky.
Follow the **lines** to work out who lives where.

BIG IS BEST

These elephants are staring into trick mirrors. Can you **spot** which mirror does **not match** its elephant?

FIND THE DINOS

Look at the dinosaurs playing in the sun. Can you **match** up each dinosaur to its **silhouette**?

BEEP, BEEP!

Five of these cars and trucks are going in a
different direction to the others. Can you **spot** them?

LEAPING DOLPHINS

The dolphins are playing in the sea. Can you **circle** the dolphin that's the **odd one out**?

SHINY CROWNS

The royal palace is full of crowns ready to be worn at the ball.

Can you **circle** the wizard's hat hidden among them?

ZERO GRAVITY

The animal astronauts are floating in space. Can you **spot six** differences between the two scenes?

SNAPPY CROCS

Count how many crocodiles are relaxing in this river scene,
then **circle** the animal friend who has come to visit them.

FISH FAMILY

These fish all swim together, but can you **find** the one with **different scales** to the rest?

WHO IS WHO?

After a party, each animal has ended up with a different baby.
Can you **match** them back into baby-and-parent **pairs**?

SPOT THE SPIDERS

These topsy-turvy spiders have grown huge!
Can you **spot** which of them is the **biggest**?

INSIDE OUT

There are **five** things in the house that belong in the **garden**, and **five** things in the garden that belong in the **house**. Can you **circle** them all?

BLOWN AWAY

It's windy out there! Can you **find** these
three umbrellas flying through the park?

FROG HOP

Help the frog hop on the lilypads by **following** them in the **order** below. He can move up, down, left and right but not diagonally.

START

FINISH

WALKIES

The dogs are getting ready to go outside. Can you **follow** the **leads** to work out which dog is joined to which thing?

FUN IN THE FIELD

Can you work out which **two** pieces **fit** where to complete the scene? **Circle** the puzzle piece that does **not** belong.

ANSWERS

Puzzle 1

Puzzle 2

Puzzle 3

Puzzle 4

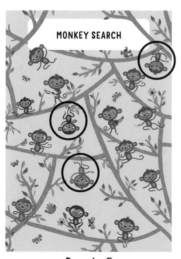

Puzzle 5

Puzzle 6

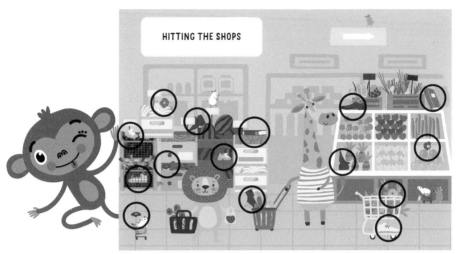

Puzzle 7

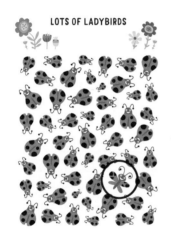

Puzzle 8

Puzzle 9

Puzzle 10

Puzzle 11

Puzzle 12

Puzzle 13

Puzzle 14

Puzzle 15

Puzzle 16

JUMPER JUMBLE

Puzzle 17

LOOP THE LOOP

Puzzle 18

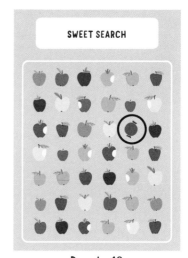

SWEET SEARCH

Puzzle 19

SCHOOLYARD SWAP

Puzzle 20

Puzzle 21

Puzzle 22

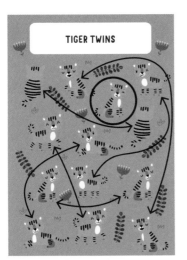

Puzzle 23

Puzzle 24

Puzzle 25

Puzzle 26

Puzzle 27

Puzzle 28

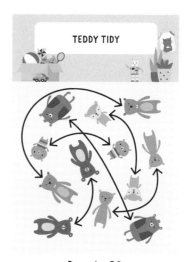

Puzzle 29

Puzzle 30

Puzzle 31

FLAMINGO FLOCK

Puzzle 32

PANDA PAIRS

Puzzle 33

AT THE CIRCUS

Puzzle 34

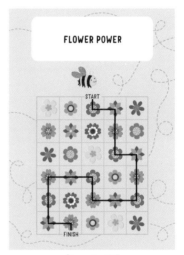

FLOWER POWER

START

FINISH

Puzzle 35

BY THE SEASIDE

Puzzle 36

Puzzle 37

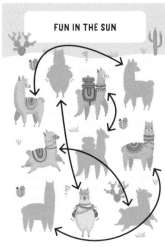

Puzzle 38

Puzzle 39

Puzzle 40

Puzzle 41

Puzzle 42

Puzzle 43

Puzzle 44

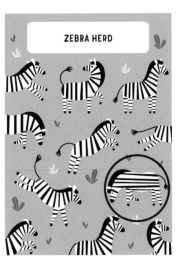

Puzzle 45

Puzzle 46

Puzzle 47

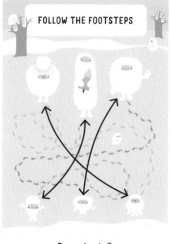

FOLLOW THE FOOTSTEPS

Puzzle 48

MOUSE HOUSE

Puzzle 49

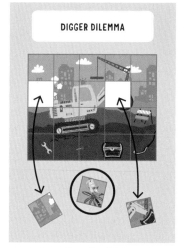

DIGGER DILEMMA

Puzzle 50

TIME FOR TEA

Puzzle 51

FOUR LITTLE PIGS

Puzzle 52

Puzzle 53

Puzzle 54

Puzzle 55

Puzzle 56

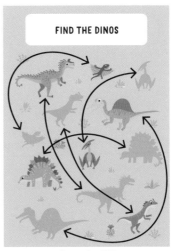

Puzzle 57

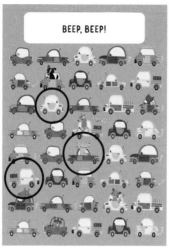

Puzzle 58

Puzzle 59

Puzzle 60

Puzzle 61

Puzzle 62

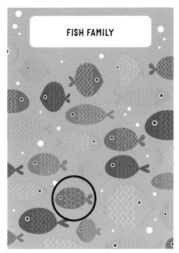

Puzzle 63

Puzzle 64

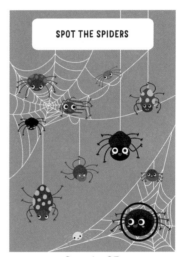

Puzzle 65

Puzzle 66

Puzzle 67

Puzzle 68

Puzzle 69

Puzzle 70